My Daddy Changed the World

My Daddy Changed the World

A Parent's and Kids Guide
to Defeat Racism

Cedric Lines

Library of Congress Control Number: 2021924068
ISBN: Hardcover   978-1-6698-0133-7
                   Softcover   978-1-6698-0131-3
                   eBook   978-1-6698-0132-0

Print information available on the last page.

Rev. date: 12/06/2021

To order additional copies of this book, contact:
Xlibris
844-714-8691
www.Xlibris.com
Orders@Xlibris.com
837128

CONTENTS

DEDICATION

This book is dedicated to the world!

We are the generation of CHANGE.
Together, we can change the world!!!

-JFK

*Together, we can uproot and
do away with racism!*

-Cedric Lines

PREVAIL OVER RACISM

I had a chance to speak with Mr. Joe Biden, before he became president. He promised me that he would do his very best to bring true and real change to our nation. Especially for the ones that are suffering and experiencing the most oppression! Now Mr. Joe, me, and my generation of change family are going to hold you to your word. And if you let us down, they are going to vote me in to be the first six-year-old president of the United States of America!

Arriana for president!

I will change the world

Chapter 1

My Daddy Changed the World

I could never forget the day that every nation, race, creed and color sprang into action.

That day, I saw the whole world while being held up high by my uncle.

Look, Uncle! Look at all these beautiful people! People that didn't possess any hate or racism; only love and peace because we are equal. On that special day, I was so joyful and proud! On that oh so beautiful day, I looked at the world and smiled. All I could say was, "My daddy changed the world!"

For my beloved daddy

Hi, my name is Arianna; and my daddy changed the world! And now, I want you all to help me to continue his legacy. We will start with the most important being of them all, GOD!

Did you know that God created you, me, and every boy and girl; man, woman, and child all equal? No matter if you are rich, poor, tall, short, big or small. It doesn't matter if you are black, brown, red, yellow, or white. We are all human beings; and we are all God's creation.

We were put in this world to respect our parents, elders, neighbors, and our friends. We were not put in this world to ridicule, mistreat, or harm each other. We must also be kind and gentle to all of God's beautiful animals. Like his dolphins and his whales that are swimming in his deep sea.

We must also be kind and gentle to God's birds that fly high in his sky, and his bees that make his sweet honey. We must take care of God's precious earth. Even His beautiful green grass and the lovely plants that grow His colorful fruits and delicious vegetables that we should always eat.

We should never pollute the water that God has provided for us to drink. Nor should we pollute God's air that we breathe.

Us and all these wonderful things come from God! He is merciful to all. So, let us be grateful to him. By being grateful to God, we will learn to love, respect, and appreciate each other. Yes, we are one big family, and the only one that is superior to us all is God!

There are no big I's or little U's. There should be no selfish Me's; only "We" or "us". We are all together. We are all one human race living under one sky, one moon, and one sun on God's beautiful earth!

Now, to the beautiful and courageous generation, who I call my family. Together, we are going to make history by making a difference. More importantly than that, we are going to make God proud of us in the process! Therefore, my aim and goal are to inspire kids of all races and from all locations around the world to strive and assist with bringing about true change. Change that can only come by ending poverty, racism, hate, and discrimination' and replacing them with honest and sincere love.

We are the ones who have to be bold and courageous enough to say that we are not racist, we are not prejudice and we are not hateful! We must show that we are loving, caring, and giving human beings who came from one source that created the whole world for us all to live in peace and harmony.

In the beginning of my book, I said, "my daddy changed the world". You may ask, Arianna, what did your daddy change about the world? And if he changed the world, why do we have to continue to change it? My Grandmother, Miss Sissy, was a spiritual and loving woman. That love continued to pour out through my dad! I guess you can say, the fruit didn't fall to far from the tree. Meaning, I have the same belief that they did; and our belief is that the only way truly change will come to the world is with God's help, and universal Love from His creations. This means love from you, me, and every living being on his planet. However, everyone hasn't accepted that love wholeheartedly. Nor have they accepted the One who possesses the ultimate power to make that change happen. That One is God Almighty! So, by me being a loving, spiritual, and intelligent little girl, I will share something of importance with you!

29:14 says, *"Blessed is the man who always fears the lord"* but he who *hardens his heart falls into trouble."*

I may be six years of age, but I can see that there are some troublesome and mean people in the world today. People with hardened hearts. Even right here in our beautiful country called America! We are going through some tough and troubling times that are not right in God's eyes. (*Need I say more?*) If you don't have the fear of God, trouble will enter your heart. Trouble will enter our schools, our playgrounds, and our households.

So, yes; we must continue to bring about change. We must continue to work towards this goal, so that trouble won't ever exist again. I'm talking about the kind of change that my daddy spread across the globe for every God-fearing human on this planet. Here is some of the change that my daddy brought to the world. He was one of God's sacrificial lambs who exposed those that have hardened hearts -which cause mischief and trouble within God's world.

My dad caused all people to see skin color as a blessing from God, and that you should be proud and accepting of it. Never hate someone because of the color of their skin. Do not think that you are better than another human being because he or she is white and you are black or vice versa.

God showed us that hate is wrong! He also showed us that all colors are beautiful in His eyes! He caused people to see that our health and wellbeing is important. That we have to eat healthy so that we can prevent disease such as diabetes, high blood pressure, obesity, among other things.

He showed us that we can love and assist those that are less fortunate, or living in poverty, those that can't afford decent housing or proper medical treatment. Those who are struggling to pay their bills and put food on the table, so that their families can eat.

He caused us to see that you shouldn't misuse or abuse people just because you are put in a position of authority. You should treat people in a righteous and fair way, for the sake of God's people that are all living together on God's earth. He showed us that all races can come together in peace and love. It's only through this unity, that we can make change for the betterment of the world! He showed us that unjust and biased laws can and will be changed. He also showed us that professional athletes, celebrities, and big tech companies can use their platforms to make a difference all around the globe. That if we unite with love and peace, we will have the power of God to bring about the change that is necessary.

So, let us use our heats, our love, and our intelligence to work together to show the rest of the world how humans are supposed to treat one another. "America is great; when we behave greatly." -Julia Jackson (Jacob Blake's Mother)

My father changed the world and I intend to keep that change growing and thriving. His death set fire to this generation; a fire that can't be extinguished, a fire that burns with justice and equality throughout the world and of course, that very same fire has created the generation of change.

<u>Generation of Change</u>

Who are we?

We are the generation to make a difference in God's world.
Spreading love, peace, and happiness to every living being which
are more precious than diamonds and pearls.

Who are we?

We are the kind hearted, loving, and innocent
Those that cannot be corrupted by racism, hatred, or ignorant.
And for those who don't know us, we will say our names.

Who are we?

We are the Generation of Change!!!

CHAPTER 2

Generation of Change

You can learn how to apply these righteous lessons that I have written just for you in your daily lives. After all, the biggest change begins within. What may begin as a chore to be worked on daily, will eventually become a beautiful part of who you are that you can be proud of.

Now that we are all reading from the same page, let's continue to display a spirit of unity and love. Keep in mind that the knowledge that we have obtained, we should gladly share with our brothers and sisters around the world.

So, are you all ready? Put on your thinking caps. Alright, let's Go!! This chapter is very near and dear to me. Because I dedicated it to the generation that walks in the image of God; in our manners as well as in our actions. Enjoining all that is good and forbidding everything that is wrong, we become examples of who God wants us to be. Meaning, we have to do all the righteous and good deeds that God likes.

While doing what's right, we shouldn't do any of the bad deeds that God dislikes. For instance, we shouldn't mistreat any of God's creations. Therefore, we must always *"Do unto to others as you would have them do unto you"* -**Matthew 7:21**

In other words, treat people how you want to be treated. Wouldn't you like to be treated with love, kindness, and respect? Of course, you would! Because, when a person gives you love, kindness, and respect… it shows that they love God and themselves. And when you love God and yourself, that makes it easier for you to love others. God loves us all. It is such a wonderful feeling when you know that you are loved by God! Why? Because we are all under the judgement of God. So, when God loves you, it shows that you are doing righteous deeds to please him. Well, you may ask, *how do we know when we are doing a rightful deed? How do you know when you are doing right by God's people? Who are God's people people?*

God's people are every human on his earth; and every human has God giving rights! What rights did God give us? God has giving us the right to breathe and live as human beings. Meaning, God gave us a right to be free on his land; and the right to be happy anywhere on His earth! Including, right here in our homeland called America. We are also given rights as citizens.

Did you say citizens, Arianna? Yes, I did. A citizen is someone who is entitled to the rights and privileges of a free person; and that free person is you, me, and every other human being. No matter their skin color or their race.

Everyone in our country is entitled to these rights as long as they were born in America. Which means, if they are born in America… then that person is an American citizen with American rights. These rights also apply to those who go through the process of naturalization-becoming a citizen through paperwork. It was our forefathers that got together and wrote the rights that the American citizens are entitled to. Who are our forefathers, Arianna? A forefather is a person of an earlier period of time.

Were these rights written for all humans black and white? If they truly wrote them with the intentions to please God, then they were written for all humans. That would mean that our forefathers knew that God Loves all and hates not one of his creations. Now on the other hand, if they wrote them for any other selfish reasons, or for one particular race or class of people… then they were written with bad intentions and do not please God!

Could people violate these rights? Yes, of course they can! When people don't live according to the constitution that was written by the forefathers -which applies to all the citizens of America, then that is certainly a violation! *So, if only Americans are entitled to these rights and privileges as a citizen, do other people throughout the world have rights as a human being as well?* Sure, they have a right to live free and be happy just like every other human being on God's beautiful earth! Just because we live here in America, doesn't mean we should think that we are better than those that are living in other countries around the world. God scattered His creations throughout the earth with different skin colors, different languages, and different features, so that one day we would realize that we are all loved by Him and therefore should love one another.

Keep in mind that if we really and truly are the generation to change the world, we must know these important things. Now let's take advantage of this knowledge, so that we can begin to change the world because changing the world is our mission!

What are the rights are we entitled to as America Citizens? Well, being an American citizen, we have so many rights. The right vote, the right to due process, and the right to be treated fairly are just a few. Some of these rights do still need adjust so that they do apply to everyone; but I will change that eventually! We should all utilize our right to vote and all of our rights. Remember, we are the generation of change, so we have to be the young voices for generations that follow. Our voices have to ring out for those that are voiceless in America, and worldwide.

"This president and those in power, those who benefit from keeping things the way they are… they are counting on your cynicism. They know they can't win you over with their policies. So, they're hoping to make it as hard as possible for you to vote and to convince you that your vote doesn't matter. We can't let that happen. Do not let them take away your power.

Don't let them take away your democracy."

-Mr. Barack Obama.

Those were Mr. Obama's words at his convention speech in his attempt to encourage people to vote for his former vice president (Joe Biden) to become our current president of the United States of America. Mr. Biden pledges to try to make this country successful with change for the betterment of God's Country and for the well-being of God's people.

However, while waiting on this change to occur, we have work to do. We cannot depend on one particular person to bring change to God's people who are suffering all over this country! So, please don't get rocked to sleep! Even though he is the chosen president for the next four to eight years, we still have to prepare ourselves for now and the near future by educating the youth (that are next in line to vote) Don't let up, tighten up!!!

It's very frustrating that I have to depend on other people to vote for things that I care about. It makes me mad. I think kids have more sense than some adults sometimes – we should be allowed to vote! But it's also important to be educated and not just follow what everyone else is doing to deter or distract you. There are lots of things you can do even if you can't vote. You can write letters. You can go to protests. You can post online to educate others. Anybody can make a difference. As long as we stay focused, we can make change happen.

"One voice is powerful. Even if you're a kid your voice is still powerful! You have to use it…"

END
SYSTEMIC
RACISM!

Voter's Education Before Registration

I have previously mentioned that we as citizens must exercise our right to vote. However, we can't put the cart before the horse. Meaning, first we must educate those that are old enough, able, and willing to vote. We must also educate the youth. Such as ourselves, who will be able to vote in the near future. This is vital to change because it is important to know why we need to vote and who we are voting for. I always hear vote, vote, vote; but I always ask myself, *why do we vote?* I also ask myself *is this person that we are voting for qualified for that position? Or is he or she really in our best interest? Is he or she really going to help us make a change for the betterment of God's People? Or are they just the average politician who is talking change and not walking it?*

People were protesting long before I was born; and they were expecting change back then. Right now, today, people are still protesting for change, as well as shouting the words, "vote, vote, vote". As I write these valuable lessons, I realize that we have four more years until the next presidential election; and I'm sad to say, we are still in desperate need of change!

Even today, we are still experiencing racism. We are still witnessing police brutality, homelessness, and poverty. These are problems that currently exist around the world and yet we have been voting to change them for generations. So, what is new? Is our ambitious and spiritual generation that has stepped out on the scene equipped with God's antidote? What is the antidote? God has blessed each and every one of His followers with love and peace -which is the cure for so many of the world's issues. Simply said, love and peace are the antidote delivered to the world with God's blessing. We will not be pacified or moved to the side, because of our age. God has given us a brain; so, we will use our minds in an intelligent way to do all positive and constructive things!

God has given us ears so that we can hear nothing but good things and ignore all that is bad or not approved by Him. He has given us a tongue, so we can speak against all forms of injustice. He has given us eyes, so we can see the unjust things that need to be corrected. He has given us a heart, so we can feel the pain of all those that suffer from mistreatment, as well as those who are facing atrocities around the world. We must learn to fight for and love all that is righteous and just! God has given us hands, so we can help the elderly and the disabled; as well as those that need a helping hand. God has given us legs, so we can walk through His earth spreading walk through His love, peace, and happiness to every human being we see. Why? Because we are the generation of change! We have been chosen and approved by God! We still have righteous and pure hearts that haven't been corrupted by ignorance or foolishness from those that wish to cause trouble in God's world. Yes, our hearts are Godly; and we are going to keep it what way. We will keep our pure and innocent hearts, which are the hearts that God gave us, despite what we see very day. We will speak the truth everywhere we go, because the truth will set us all free.

Our primary goal is to speak the truth to falsehood. *What is falsehood?* It means something that is untrue. So, the truth is, we must become fully aware and inepter with issues such as racism. We must be mindful of the hate and the pain and suffering that racism has caused to God's people. First of all, we are not too young to know about these unjust and ungodly terms, racism and hate. Nor are we too young to notice the harm that is caused to God's people by them. Of course, knowing the meaning of these ungodly words will educate us with these horrible facts of life. That knowledge will prepare us for our future; so, that we won't have a blind eye to what exists in the world today. Furthermore, the level of boldness that these atrocities are being committed have become too much to ignore.

Now, I would like to address all the parents that are listening. Please be open minded, because you can learn from all of God's Creations, even a six-year-old!

Every parent has given birth to a precious gift from heaven! Yes, we are God's precious creations and a gift to you. Did you know that a baby is innocent at birth, with no traits of racism, biasness, or hate and that a child is upright by nature? That is why we as kids don't have hate in our hearts. These individual traits are taught or instilled in a child by its parents. Or picked up through bad influence from family, friends, television, the internet, or even school. With that said, we must do inventory on ourselves, to see if we possess any form of hate or racism. This must start with the parents (white or black).

Ask yourself, *do I harbor any form of hate in my heart towards another race or color?* Or ponder this in your thoughts. *Was it taught to me by my parents -who may have learned it from their parents? Did I get it from my friends or my significant other? Did I hear it on television?* And most importantly, *did I pass it down to my child knowingly or unknowingly?* Only through self—reflection can we pinpoint and begin to correct these traits within ourselves.

Now, back to my generation of change family. We as kids have to be extra careful not to pick up those evil traits. However, if you are victim of this evil disease, please know that you are not alone or beyond change. The vicious disease called racism has become a pandemic and I'm sorry to say this, but God's beautiful nation called America is experiencing the deadliest infection. You may ask, *is there a cure for this ugly disease?* My answer to your question would be… absolutely, without a doubt! First and foremost, God is the ultimate solution to the massive and horrific pandemic that we are experiencing. He is the cure of all cures. I will quote what my Daddy uses to say to his "little angel". "Faith without works is no good!"

We must show faith in our actions and God will do the rest. Remember this! With active unity and the good Lord by our side, we will rid this world of racism. We will use every Godly and positive tool at our disposal to achieve this much needed goal. We are utterly convinced of the righteousness of our cause because we truly believe that God is with those that do right by Him and all of His creations. "It's not going to take a miracle; it's going to take God" -To end structural racism

The hate that is being waged on our country is escalating daily; and it won't deescalate until we sincerely put God in our hearts as well as our minds. We must also put God in our homes, our schools and universities, our jobs, our neighborhoods (urban and suburban) and upscale areas alike. We must spread the love of God in the hearts of our City Hall officials.

We must put the Love of God in the hearts of our City Councils, our Mayors, and our Governors. We must put God in the Pentagon, in our National Guard, our prison system, in our police stations and unions, and in our hospitals as well as in our court rooms. We have to put God in our Military and in the Department of Justice. We must put God in our Appeals courts, our District courts, all the way up to our Supreme Court. We need God in our Treasury Department, in our banks, our congress, our white house, and the United Nations. By putting God in these places, and in the hearts as well as the minds that govern these places, it will allow God's people to begin to have righteous and just belief in the decision making and judgment of His people in those positions. Because without God present with His just commandments or laws… liberty and justice will not be righteously served to those that yearn for their freedom and equality. Without God present, we will continue to pack jails and prisons with no form of rehabilitation. We will continue to see wars and hearing rumors of wars. We will continue to see human rights violations all around the world without accountability. We will continue to see black on black crimes; and we will continue to see hate crimes! We will continue to see police brutality and global protests against racial injustice. We will continue to see discrimination in our schools and at our jobs. We will continue to see racial inequality, unemployment, and biasness in our courtrooms and in our banks. We will continue to see the rich get richer while the poor get poorer. We will continue to see improvised neighborhoods, homelessness, and poverty throughout America. So, we must get to the root cause of all these detrimental things that have caused the human race to live ungodly on God's earth. Because without unity and the love for God in His people. We will not prosper as a nation under God!!! And yes Family, this will take all of us. This means every human on God's planet. Starting right here in America. We must work together on one united front, with the old and the young. It is very important for us as minors to receive that wise advice from those that are much older than we are, lending us a helping hand to build a better tomorrow for our generation and the generation to comes after us.

I am more than happy and proud to stand alongside those that are with the generation of change in building a brighter, more just, and prosperous future that we as God's children rightfully deserve. No more depriving us of our humanity. Change for all people is unquestionable. My daddy's honor and my words will not go in vain. My love and my adoration for my father has no limits! My father's love as well as his passion for all people was evident! Therefore, the torch has been passed to his youngest seed. And as I grow, the world will grow with me. We will grow into the love of Go and go further than any of those that came before us ever imagined. We will grow into the love for humanity. We will grow into peace, happiness, and prosperity. Finally, we will grow into unconditional love, and that unconditional love will conquer the world! With the power that highlights the ungodly things that we need to change.

I will expose the ungodly things that we need to change as a country and the people that live in it. With God in all of our affairs, we will reform ourselves and once more obtains God's favor. Now, Let's continue this Godly mission called change!

It's obvious that the changes we need are structural. Elected officials that govern this structural system lack the fear of God! So, with their selfish desires, they hand pick who they feel are entitled to their just do rights. This ugly monster called racism has remained deeply planted into the American system and must be rooted out now and forever! This is why God's people are looked down on and mistreated by others in America- because of the way we are treated by our officials. Arrogance has caused them to become disobedient to God; and when you are disobedient to God, you no longer respect all the righteousness and good that God stands for -which is justice, peace, equality, happiness, and most importantly love! These are all Godly and righteous things that we as God's creations should possess in our hearts, as well as in our minds. And most importantly, we must express these in our actions towards others! Furthermore, when those who mistreat others out of ignorance or arrogance and their ungodly ways have replaced those just and Godly things that we are naturally born with, for mischief and hate, people to do hateful things on God's beautiful earth! At the same time, spreading mischief throughout His land without the fear of God, shows that only an enemy of God will deprive another human being of what God intended for that human being to have.

"All Human beings are born equal in dignity and rights." – Philonise Floyd Justice applies equally to all; regardless of their creed, class, or color. This has led me to my next question; and this question has been lingering in the minds of some of my white family ever since this movement has been in existence. *Why do black lives' matter and not white lives? When you say black lives matter, does that mean other lives don't matter?* Of course not! Each and every human being that walks on God's green earth matters. Not only do all lives matter, but all lives deserve to exist without injury or harm. However, black lives are the ones who are suffering the most; we have endured tremendous misery and distress! Black lives are the ones that are treated the worst. Black Lives are the ones that are being deprived of justice, liberty, and equality -which bring on love, peace, and happiness!

Be mindful that when I say black lives, I mean African Americans,

Latin Americans, Asian Americans, and Native Americans. Those who have a darker skin complexion… like I do. They are the people that are being discriminated against and mistreated on a daily basis. Those are the people that are being harassed and abused by police, while up against systemic racism. These are the people that are looked down on by people in a higher class, out of arrogance or simply because they do not care for God's people. This is why Black lives are more of a priority, as opposed to those that are still God's people but are not experiencing these harsh and ungodly things. There are some poor white lives that are subjected to these harsh conditions as well! So yes, this is an emergency for us as a suffering people!

For example, if two people go to the emergency room for their injuries; one of those people has a little scratch that obviously needs a band aid, and the other has a big ugly cut that requires stitches… which person do you think that the doctor will care for first? The one that has the scratch or the one that has the more serious injury? Of course, the doctor would care for the person that need the stitches because their injury is much more severe -which could become life threatening! Honestly speaking, that is the situation with black lives. We are suffering the more serious injuries. Keep in mind that our injuries are not just "boo boo's", or superficial. Our cuts are deep lacerations caused by injustice, systemic racism, and deep-rooted hatred! These wounds have been hurting the minority communities for centuries. So, this is why black lives matter! This is why people are protesting worldwide. I am talking countless people of all colors and races. People have united to bring about true justice. Not only for those who are experiencing injustice in America, but also those who are suffering similar injuries in other countries around the world. These wounds can only be healed by the knowledge of truth and justice done in accordance of that truth. So, by acknowledging the truth… you have opened your heart and minds to God's mercy and grace for his suffering and oppressed people. So, yes, every culture has its aches and ailments… black lives deserve to be prioritized. With that said, I sincerely ask those who have Godly hearts and minds to join forces with the generation of change family so that we can passionately work together as one to fore fill the highest ideas of our founders, that we are all created equal and we deserve equal treatment according to the constitution of America. Change is a much-needed Godly force in a nation that's already traumatized by disease, disaster, and division. And for those who turn a deaf ear to the mistreatment and abuse of God's people, as if to say, the hand shall not lend aid when the eye is suffering… we all are one body that has one heart -which were all created by one God under one nation.

I am god's creation, so I have a right to live!

I am a human, so I have human rights!

I am a citizen, so I must be treated as one!

Arianna Floyd – For America

Remember this: He who reads will learn, and he who learns should teach. And by teaching, we could share our knowledge of how to enact change. Together, we can begin to make God's world a better place! *What is change?* Change is to make a difference. Change is to give a different position, course, or direction to. Therefore, we should become leaders in order to make this change occur. It will be hard for a leader to guide with no direction. This is why together we must create a plan, so that we will know the directions to go in on our path to make change our destination. Then we can begin to make the world a better place.

In order for us to change, first we must want change. Then you have to plan change, then we begin living out what we have planned. Here is an example on how to change. We know how much kids love candy, don't we? Let's pretend that one day a kid learns that the sugar that is in candy is very bad for him, and that sugar could cause his teeth to decay. After hearing how bad candy is, he plans to change the way he eats. So, he decides to stop eating candy. Then he begins to eat foods that are healthy for him like fruits, vegetables, and nuts. That is how we make change one step at a time, with that step leading into the step to be taken.

You see! While coming from different cultures creates some differences among us, we have some similarities as well. Our goals, our dreams, our passions make all people lovely and ambitious to aspire others be great. In this way, all colors are beautiful!

Here are three easy steps to making change.

1. First, you have to want change.
2. Next, we plan the change.
3. Last, you must live out your desire to experience change.

We can use those three easy steps when making change because change can't continue to be only something we talk about. Change must be lived in order for change to happen!

What is your plan to change something in God's world for the wellbeing of his people, as well as his animals? Please write your answer on the lines provided below.

____

____

____

____

____

____

____

____

Questions for America

Being the curious and inquisitive little girl that I am, I have some critical questions for America that must be answered! I will start with:

1. What is a united nation if those that deserves human rights never receives it?
2. Why is there a constitution, when constitutional rights for all people only apply to some?
3. What is the purpose for congress when they never get along when it comes to passing meaningful laws for the betterment of God's people?
4. Why are there blue states and red states and not the United States?
5. Why do we have the white house when a president puts politics and economics over the wellbeing of the American citizens?
6. Why do we have attorney generals if they are going to continue to turn a deaf ear every time it's time to bring charges for hate crimes such as lynching and police brutality
7. What is the purpose of having a supreme court when out of the thousands of cases being filed, only a few or so cases are lucky to be heard, while the remaining cases are usually rubber stamped by the clerk of courts. Especially prisoner's Appeals!
8. Why do we have a police station when the police only protect a certain race and class of people?
9. Why do we have a police union when the union always justifies the wrong that the police do to its citizens who they are supposed to protect and serve?

10. What is the reason for having schools when only the rich or well-off kids are the only ones to receive a proper and decent education while the public-school students get second-hand education, and are forced to learn from outdated books and computers?

11. What's the use of having teachers when they never get paid a decent salary for their good deeds and services?

12. What's the use of having banks when a certain race or class are always discriminated against?

13. What's the use of having a mosque, a church, or a synagogue when it's not safe to praise God?

14. What is the need for a Grand Jury, when those in authority commit a racist or hateful act never get indicted?

15. Why do we have judicial system when prisoners have to fight tooth and nails just to get a case made retroactive or overturned by a judge, When the merits of their case display obvious violation of the defendant's constitutional rights?

16. Why do we have a district court when racism and biasness play a major role in sentencing minorities more severe than their white counterparts?

Last and certainly not least, for those who say out of ignorance why do "black lives matter" well,

17. Why are your life and limb, your property and honor so free and mine are not, when we are all human beings under God's law but when it comes to human law… we are not American?

Chapter 3

All Colors Are Beautiful

One day we will no longer be labeled by the color of our skin but by the contents of our heart.

All colors are beautiful, all colors are bright

When it comes to skin color, there's no wrong or right
Because God don't make mistakes

With the colors of the humans that He creates So, why judge a person for the color of their skin When we all have the same heart within?

Arianna Floyd, **All Colors are beautiful**

We cannot change the reality in which we are born. None of us had any say whatsoever over how God shaped and molded us into the precious human beings that we are. Furthermore, we didn't decide the beautiful color that God chose for us to be. If we truly love and trust in God, we will appreciate and accept all of his lovely creations just the way they are. I am more than grateful of the way God made me. Thank you, God; for the wonderful work that you have done!

Are you all thankful for how God made you and all the wonderful people in the world? If the answer is yes, then you all are so on point!

Being thankful for the way God made you, as well as appreciating his creations of others, clearly shows that you are Godly, caring, and loving to yourselves and to God's people! By us being aware of these righteous things, we can proudly say that all colors are beautiful and pleasant to the eye. All shapes and sizes are well put together; and can be used for righteous and good deeds on God's earth. All languages are unique and eloquent and can be voices of change. All names that your parents named you are nice names! Everything about who you are, every piece that makes the whole you are perfect.

Take myself for instance. My parents gave me the name Arianna; and I am African American. I am "Black" and my ancestors are from Africa. I was born in America and birthed by two loving and wonderful parents!

My beloved father's name was George; and my lovely mother's name is Roxie. Both of them, I love and cherish daily! Every part of who they are is a piece of who I am and will somehow shape who I become.

My father was 6 foot 3 inches tall and weighed 223 pounds. I know that you are saying to yourself, "wow"! And I agree, he was a big guy. God blessed him to be big and strong. Just like the great Solomon who was one of God's righteous prophets, my father also did so many wonderful things with his structure and size. For instance, my cousin Brooke said my father was her favorite uncle. Brooke also said that he was like "superman to her" because my daddy was heroic. She was amazed at how he would lift my disabled grandmother out of her specially made van with ease without a bit of strain! In the blink of an eye, my grandmother would be in the confines of her home safe and sound, just like that. Courtesy of my dad, the world super hero! He was also known as a selfless man who would take homeless people to the medical appointments and basketball games. His heart was just as big as his stature.

Unfortunately, color played a major part in my father's demise! In fact, color has caused the lives of countless others as well. I send my deepest condolences to the families that have lost a loved one all because God chose them to be a different color or race. Please know that they are in a special place called heaven, where all colors are beautiful and pleasant in the sight of the One who perfectly colored them.

Heaven is a safe and secured place where my father could be with his mother without any worries of harassment or harm. It's a place where my father can breathe freely for an eternity. Without the fear of losing his breath from those that wish to cut it short. My father is in place where my grandmother is no longer disabled and she can walk hand-in-hand with her son without him having to carry her in his arms. It's in a place where the Almighty God Himself is looking over His universe in which we live to see if we are all getting along together as one loving and caring family.

We so easily forget the purpose for which we were created. To praise him in all ways possible- which includes how we treat one another. Praising God is the sole purpose that He created us in the first place. Now, how often do we forget to praise Him? How could we fulfill our obligations to God when we are disobedient to Him, and cruel and mean to His creations? We must fulfill our duties to God by being grateful servants. If not, we will continue to harbor hate in our hearts; and the hate that we conceal comes out in ways that can be harmful to God's creations.

This can never be said too loudly, or repeated too often. Never Judge or dislike someone because judging someone for the color of their skin out of pride, anger, arrogance, or envy is not Godlike.

Aren't we supposed to be godly and righteous people? We are supposed to fulfill our duties and sincerely be devoted to the One who created us. If you are truly trying to please God, and walk in a righteous manner on His earth… you must control your prideful thoughts and lead with love in all your actions. You must do a self-check and ask yourself these questions. *Why do I think I am better than my brothers and sisters?* Yes, I said brothers and sisters, because that is what we are. We all came from God's first creation. Therefore, we are all one big family, striving to please the almighty God! I know that you are probably wondering if we are all one family striving to please God, then why do we have people that still do hateful things to others? Things such as systemic racism, oppression, verbal or physical abuse? Well, this isn't a hard question to answer. People mistreat others out of ignorance -the lack of knowledge of God and knowledge of themselves. Once you truly know who God is and what He created you for -your designed purpose in life, then you will begin to know yourself. When you know yourself, you will learn to love, respect, and appreciate others. Then you will begin to recognize that all of God's creations are beautiful! That being a different color or race is not a crime. Remember, we are not irredeemably evil creatures or devilish by nature. We can be forgiven by a forgiving and a merciful God. When you turn to Him in repentance, and submit to Him with sincerity, He will indeed answer your prayers. That is, for those who have reached the age to know right from wrong.

That's why this is so important for parents to know! We as kids need that Godly guidance from our love ones at an early age. If we are taught right from wrong at a beginning stage in our lives, then we will grow with those same morals and principles to be Godlike when we are much older.

This was profoundly written in God's scriptures.

Proverbs 22:5-*Train a child in the way he or she should go, and when they are old, they will not turn from it.*

It is very important for us to know that we are the next generation to enter the racist and unbalanced structures in our society. We will enter a society where biasness and prejudices are running ramped. We will enter a society where discrimination by those that look down on people of color have become the norm in places where authority has been misused and abused. This is not only important for our African American kids, but this is also significant for the kids who are in our Caucasian family as well. We must unify our hearts and minds in a Godly way to rid this ugly monster that has God's people at odds because of color!

We can do it, family! We have to because we are the generation of change. We don't have any bias or hate in our hearts and minds yet. We have to start to create and build this change now. So, our parents will not teach us those things. They have to know that they are God's vessel to give us the righteous guidance that we so rightfully deserve as God's little Angels.

We are living in a time where whites and Blacks are uniting like never before; and are protesting all around the country. They are coming together on football fields, on basketball courts, black and white people are coming together in college on campus, and they are sharing dorm rooms and apartments. My white friends and I play on the playground together. We also have sleepovers that are so much fun!

We are not living in black and white anymore. We are living a life in which colors are blossoming into something oh so beautiful! This is how God's world is supposed to be. His world was designed to have multiple colors, languages, and races in it. Animosity towards each other shouldn't exist. Now, we can proudly say that God gave each individual different skin colors for a reason, and God knows best, right? Who knows better than God? The answer is no one.

I want you all to think for a minute. Are your thinking caps still on? Alright, let's go! Just picture if God decided to make everything and everybody the same. How do you think the world would look? Imagine everything black! Imagine everything white, red, orange, or green. Picture you, me, and everyone on God's earth being the same color. Wow! One solid color. How bland and plain and less interesting would that be? Wouldn't that look weird, boring, or dull? Now just imagine if God made every one of us to look just alike. I'm talking identical, with all the same features. Better yet, picture God making us talk alike. Wouldn't that be strange if we all spoke the same language with the same voice? Don't you like how your voice sounds? Don't you love how beautiful your skin color is? It doesn't matter if your skin is black, brown, white, red, or yellow, it was created by God. Every unique and wonderfully made thing about each and every one of us was absolutely intentional. I can't imagine it ever being any other way.

Our differences are what makes us unique and beautiful beings. Even Gods animals are unique and beautiful. Look at all the exotic colors that God has blessed them with. Take the zebra for instance, it has the most amazing black and white stripes! Look at the giraffes and their unique colors. Look at the colorful birds that God created like the blue Jays, red robins, or His multi-colored parrots. Look at the brightly colored fish that God create. You would easily identify these as God's beautiful creatures with different shapes, colors, and sizes. The one thing they all have in common is their beauty. Wouldn't you agree?

I have some questions that I would like for you all to answer on the lines below. Remember family, I expect you all to give an honest answer. This is for your growth, no one else are not going to judge you or your answers. Only God has the right to do that.

1. Do you think that all colors are beautiful, and if so, why?

    ____

2. What are your favorite colors?

    ____

    ____

3. Do you love all God's creations?

    ____

    ____

4. What do you love the most in God's creations?

____

____

I love all of God's beautiful colors. It makes His world lovely and bright. I have friends of all colors and races. I have friends of all races and backgrounds. Some of them are Latinos, Africans, Asians, Indians, Arabians, and so on. I love them all the same.

How about you? Do you have friends of different races and all colors? Do you love them all the same? Write the races that your friends are, as well as their names

____

____

If you have embraced friends of different backgrounds, then you have pleased God. You are loved and adored by Him as well. God has created you and your friends to all have love and respect for one another no matter what color or race you are. Remember, all colors are a blessing from God. Because without the colors that God has put into the world, beauty and brightness wouldn't exist.

Thanks to God, and the fact that He loves His creations so much, we have been blessed with all those that makes this life wonderful. Now, please allow me to share something with my family. I have a dog name Cinderella and she is snow white. Do any of you have a pet? If so, what are their names, and what colors are they?

"I have a_______ and his or her name is __________"

However, if you so happen not to own a pet then that's okay because every animal in God's creations is your pet. So, love them and take care of them all -so God can love and care for you, for loving and caring for all His creations. It's this love that will bring about the change that so needed in our society today.

Remember! Never judge a book by its cover. Read it to find out what it's all about. Never judge a person by the color of their skin. First, you should get to know a person by judging their heart as well as that person's actions. Actions from a loving and caring heart are what adds brightness to the world. Showing Love over hate is what distinguishes you as one of God's people. So, let your loving light shine!

Chapter 4

Love Over Hate

"No matter what color or race you are, we all want to see better days. So, we must spread more love than hate" – Lebron James -one of the greatest basketball players on the planet!

Hate is a virus and love are the cure we create. So, together let's spread love all over the world starting with putting an end to poverty and hunger. With love, America and her fifty states, we can feed the poor, the hungry, and the homeless all off one big plate!

With love, we can end arguments, fights, and wars.

With the love and peace, we make…

We can defeat the barriers that have caused so much suffering and pain from the tragedy's we face.

Yes, with love we will change the world!!! Making it a safe and loveable place!

-Arianna Floyd, Love Over Hate

In this special chapter, we must pay very close attention family. In this chapter, lies a solution to all of our ongoing trouble that hate has caused the people in America, as well as the people throughout the world. You may ask, *what could possibly conquer hate?* The answer is none other than God's extraordinary antidote called love! We must put love into our atmosphere. We must put it back into our homes, schools, playgrounds, as well as our neighborhoods, and all across the globe. In order to do these Godly things, first we must educate ourselves on what love truly is. So, let's start with what God said -which is written in His wonderful scripture!

Corinthians 14:4 God said that love is patient, love is kind. It does not envy, it does not boast, it isn't proud. It isn't rude. It isn't self-seeking, it isn't easily angered. It keeps no record of wrongs. Love doesn't delight in evil, but rejoices with the truth; always hopes, always perseveres.

And there is so much more to love. Now that you know some of what God said love is, let's talk a little bit about what hate is.

Hate is the opposite of love.

Hate is to dislike! Hate is anger!

Hate is to destroy!

Hate is Evil!

Hate is Bad!

Hate is Selfish!

Hate is being mean and evil to God's creations!

However, hate gives us all a reason to love, because sometimes the things that we hate the most… could be the best things for us.

Think about this… Has someone ever cooked you a meal with vegetables on the plate; and when you began to eat the vegetables, you hated how they taste? Well, did you all know that those same vegetables that we hate to eat has the vitamins, nutrients and all the good things that our bodies need to grow healthy and strong. They have the nutrients we need to grow up and become the leaders the world needs our generation to be?

Now think about this… Have you ever been at home and when you looked out the window, you noticed that it was pouring down raining? Because of the rain, you weren't allowed to go outside and play with your friends. When that happen, did you say to yourself, I hate when it rains? Well, you need to know that when God made it rain, He was watering His beautiful earth. So, those same vegetables that you hated to eat could grow; and this way you would always have the vegetables that you need to stay healthy and strong. We really need to start eating our vegetables! God takes his time to make sure that the best things for us are there for us to enjoy. That is one of the reasons I said sometimes the things that we hate the most, can be the best things for us.

On the other hand, hate has caused a lot of bad things to happen! Hate has caused a lot of us to make bad choices. Like not eating out vegetables, or not caring for God's creations. We mistreat God's people as well as all the things that we should love. Always remember that to hate is to not care, and if we don't care, we won't be kind. If you are not kind, you won't share. If you don't share, you won't give…. and if we don't give, we won't love.

If we are going to make the world a better place, we must start by giving love to one another, because love will cure hate. If everyone in the world were to love, then hate wouldn't exist. So, now is the time to start loving.

This love that I passionately speak of family, is God's solution to the very hate that causes deep rooted racism. Yes, this is that horrible monster that we've talked about! Generally speaking, hate is infecting our society, our police departments, our court houses, our white house, our congress, and even our homes. We are being pacified with the falsehood that hate and racism are dead and gone. The truth is, hate and its best friend racism are alive and well; and is causing havoc without any form of love to defeat it. It's literally killing us; but there's no need to panic. *Why?* Because we are here to say no more! No more racism or hate will ever exist on our watch. We are the generation to reintroduce love to the world! For those who are in doubt of our mission to spread God's love, I know that you are wondering how can you love somebody that you don't know? Easy! If you love God, then you will love all in which He created. How can you love someone that clearly has hate for you? Again, easy. It is God's command to do so.

Even those that are on the other side of God's planet have hearts just like the ones beating inside your chest and mine. Therefore, if someone is being mistreated in Africa, you should feel love for them. If someone is being abused in London, China, Australia, Italy, or anywhere on God's beautiful earth, you should feel love and compassion for them. They are all part of God's creations. No matter what part of the world they live in. Nor does it matter what race or color they are. They are human beings with a heart like yours and mine. This is why we are spreading love all across the country and abroad. We are spreading love to men, women, and children that are oppressed and living in impoverished areas around the world crying because they don't have enough food to eat, nor do they have shoes to put on their feet. We are spreading love to those who don't have a bed to sleep in, or close on their backs. We are spreading love to those who don't have a roof over their thread, or clean water to drink. We are also spreading love to those that are crying out and praying for someone to come and rescue them from the pain and suffering as well as the poverty that has countless people in a state of despair!

One may say, *aren't we experiencing similar atrocities and hardship right here in America?* That is true! By me being a six-year-old righteous fighter for justice, I can't box with the truth; but just like my good friend's grandfather Dr. Martin Luther king Jr. once believed that an injustice in one place is also an injustice everywhere else. So, we must recognize if one of God's human beings are suffering, then the whole of His human race has suffered likewise. So, if you have a Godly heart, a compassionate heart, or a loving heart, then you shouldn't turn a deaf ear to the abuse or oppression that has continued to take place on God's earth. Furthermore, America can't hide the mistreatment that has been waged upon God's people! The things that are occurring around the world are noticeable even for someone that's my age.

I am no stranger to the hate that God's people are up against right here in the land of the so called "free"; and I certainly don't pretend to be. Why should I, if I really and truly want to grow up and change the world? We must learn where this hate lies, so that we can apply love where it's needed. Love is the cure to root out this disease that is threatening to swallow the world. Be mindful that this is a new generation and time. God has opened our eyes. We are spiritually conscious. So, our vision is clear. We can see the bad and wrong things that are happening today with no shame or remorse. It is God's people that are enduring these unnecessary hardships. Especially, people of color who are the usual victims of abuse by police. Convictions are few and far between for the perpetrators. Hate has provoked widespread protests calling for change. People are calling for change of systemic racism, police brutality, and structural equalities. People are protesting against stereotyping and profiling just because of a person's skin color. It's no secret that racial discrimination has made it harder for people of color to succeed, let alone breathe in America! So, by me being a young African American, living in America where hate is bred, I must prepare myself to meet those ungodly truths. I will be equipped with God's antidote to defeat them and this is all backed by God Almighty as well as my generation of change family.

This is why I am certain that we are on a righteous path to bring nothing but love to God's nation. We are fully aware that God is the all-seeing eye! God hears, sees, and knows everything. So, nothing we do goes unnoticed by God. Therefore, we must always display good manners as well as be on our best behavior! I can say with much confidence that I will please God with nothing but deeds of righteousness, in addition to hoping and praying that we can help the world love, all while bringing to light the craft and deceit of the devil.

God gave us that word so that we will be fully aware of the devil and his knavish and crafty deceptions to keep us at odds. Young or old, we are no stranger to the devil and his wickedness! That is if you are reading the holy scriptures as God commands us to. If you are reading those scriptures, then it is perfectly clear who the devil is, as well as his sole mission on earth. So, for those who don't know, allow me to take you all to church.

The devil was once a servant of God, that dwelled in God's kingdom! While in God's kingdom, the devil was accompanied by God's sinless angels, and his righteous creations Adam and Eve. However, the devil became disobedient to God when God told his Angels to prostrate themselves to Adam. Yes, with humbleness and discipline, they prostrated themselves; but not the devil. He refused out of arrogance. All because he believed that he was better than God's creations. So, in a way… the devil himself possessed racism.

God disciplined him by removing him from the kingdom of heaven, and by God being so merciful, he answered the devil's request to remain on God's earth until his time is up. Now he is roaming around on God's earth trying his very best to tempt you, me, and the whole world to be disobedient to God, exactly like he did.

"I will come from the side the front the back and tempt them all."

The devil can deceive us by whispering into our ears, trying to encourage us to choose hate over love. Yes family, that is how the devil works; and his handiwork will not stop until he corrupts us with arrogance. That arrogance will turn into racism; that racism will turn into hate. Then that hate will certainly destroy the world! Fortunately, we have God's blessings and His protection.

Despite minor mistakes, we are still in our purest form, created by God and our purity has not been tainted in any form or fashion. So, for those who fall into temptation by the devil, you must continue to ask God to guide you through the valley where the hate lies, while rebuking all that is evil, because we are not perfect. God said if He were to punish for every wrong or shortcoming, not a single living creature on earth would escape punishment; but with God's infinite mercy and forgiveness, He gives respite and a chance to sincerely ask for forgiveness. He provides time for repentance. So, for those who have committed a crime should not be judged by man if they have sincerely asked God for forgiveness, and have paid their debt to society for their crimes. Whatever that crime may be, God will forgive them. So, should the Judicial system -who should be in the business of advocating for rehabilitation instead of incarceration.

God's generation of change will proudly say "no" to crime in any form, shape, or fashion. Also, we will gladly say "no" to drugs, because it is detrimental to our growth and development! However, we shouldn't look down on, nor judge, those that are addicted to drugs because God knows that the flesh is weak so He offers the strength of prayer!

Because of God's love for us, all prays go to Him; and He is in the highest position of authority. Keep in mind that God's authority exceeds all human beings here on earth. Those who are aware of the power of God should always love, respect, and pray to Him. Theism raises the question, why don't those that God has allowed to have minor positions of authority on his earth have the same forgiveness, compassion, or love that God has? Why do they continue to mistreat God's people by abusing them with their cruel and usual brutality? Then they justify their ungodly actions by referring to themselves as the victim with intentions to discredit or dehumanize the actual victim. Or they will claim that they were in fear of their life when unnecessary or excessive force is used, when in fact they were power struck and controlling!

Family, it's sad; but it's true! Remember when I said that you may hate some things that are good for you? Well, a lot of people hate the truth! Now, I must quote my beloved father. He would say, "You should always speak the truth and shame the devil." Therefor family, we are never too young or too old to speak the truth, even though ungodly people hate it. If they only knew, it's good for them! Those that possess hate or racism in their hearth are indeed worthy to be given another chance to change their behavior or mindset. Individuals that are sincerely seeking redemption, could put their bad past behind them and have a fresh start in life. If God is forgiving, then we must be forgiving as well. We are God's people, who shouldn't be agents of the devil. When the world sees that we are walking in righteousness, even the haters will recognize and speak about how we are none other than the obedient ones of God! Racism is ugly and sad and love is always happy and beautiful just like we are. So, let's continue to plant seeds of happiness and love in the world; this will bring forth the fruits of righteousness in our hearts and minds.

We have Choose Love Over Hate. Below is a list of some of the things that some people hate:

-Some people hate snakes!
-Some people hate rats!
-Some people hate spiders!
-Some people hate vegetables!
-Some people hate cats!
-Some people hate ants!

Did you know that God created all things for a reason, including the things that people hate? Which means, God didn't create snakes, rates, spiders, vegetable, cats, or ants for us to hate. All of God's creations are for us to Love. Remember, hate is a virus, but love is the vaccine. Hate is energy wasted. This is why we should always try to Love. And the things that you can't learn to love, you should pray to God to change your heart. Never hate what you can't learn to love, because hate is causing people to destroy God's world!

Hate has cause Racism!
Hate has caused Pain!
Hate has caused destruction!
But!
Love will cure Racism!
Love will cure sickness!
Love will rebuild destruction

This is why we should always put love over hate. Before I end this chapter, I thought that it was very important that I share with you all my idea on how we can begin to spread love, so that we could end hate. After you read this book, tell whoever you are around that you love them. Tell that person to tell someone else that they love them as well; and that person should tell the next person that they love them. This should go on until love begins to spread like wildfires! Instead of the destruction that wildfires cause, your love will spread peace and happiness all around the world! Now let's begin to spread our love and defeat hate because I know every one of you have a heart of gold.

We need the heart to

We need the heart to

We need the heart to

We need the heart to

The heart is pure, the heart is

The heart is precious, it is a heart

Chapter 5

Hearts of Gold

God is so merciful that he blessed us with one of his precious creations! He gave us a heart. Did you know that we need a heart to function in more ways than you could imagine? For instance, we need the heart to breathe, we need a heart to feel, we need a heart to see, we need a heart to walk and talk. Without the heart, the human body wouldn't exist; and without the heart, we couldn't love. This is why we must cherish our precious hearts; and we must also take good care of our hearts.

How do we take good care of our hearts? First, we have to do right by the heart by giving God thanks for creating it just for us! By giving God thanks, you are showing Him that you appreciate what He has done for us, out of love and mercy for His creation. Once you acknowledge that it's a blessing to have God's heart, then you will begin to take good care of the heart. You will also begin to apply the good and wholesome things that the heart needs. Yes, the heart needs you as well as you need your heart. Meaning, if you give it good and Godly things, it will give you good and Godly things in return. In case you are wondering what are the good and godly things for the heart, I am more than willing to inform you of what those good and godly thins will consist of. First, I will start with God; because He has been extremely good to us by blessing us with His precious heart! So of course, we must put God first. With God in our hearts, we will continuously desire the things that are righteous in order for the heart to remain good and Godly. Next on my list of Godly things is love -which I spoke so passionate about in the previous chapter! Furthermore, love is the second thing we should always possess in our hearts because love is gentle. Love is kinds, and love will keep the heart good and godly throughout the test of time. Third, we have to put the love of God's people inside the heart because they are those that are good and kind to Him. Yes family, God's people are the ones that love and recognize the blessings God gives just like we do. We have to give love and goodness back to them. So, it is safe to say that you have to put care in your hearts because you are supposed to love and care for all of God's creations. All of this is good for the heart. It keeps the heart loving; it keeps the heart kind. It causes the heart to give, it allows the heart to be free from things that are bad for it!

Things like hate, racism, or doing wrong things to other with similar hearts that are godly like ours. Just as importantly, the heart requires God's good and wholesome foods. Goods such as God's lean clean meats, nuts, fruits, and those good ole vegetables that I told you about earlier! Remember when I said that vegetables "will make us healthy and strong to become the young leaders for the world? Yes family, God's good and wholesome foods keep the heart that He blessed us with pumping healthy and strong. Let me give you some nutritional knowledge. It's good nutrients, protein, and vitamins in God's good and wholesome foods aside from eating those delicious vegetables, which are supremely good for us as well. Now I mentioned lean and clean meats; but I never told you what kind. For instance, baked or grilled turkey, fish, or chicken has plenty of protein that is good for the heart. Baked and grilled because when it's baked or grilled, it's better for the heart as opposed to frying it with grease or cooking oil -which can be bad for the heart. If mommy decides to fry it, at least you can suggest to her in a kind and nice way to fry it in healthy oils, such as olive oil and almond oil.

For your information, there are a lot more wholesome and godly things for the heart, like fruits. Fruits such as God's oranges, apples, grapes, bananas, peaches, kiwis, mangos, strawberries, plums, and pears. And that was just to name a few. In addition to that information, God's vegetables are also healthy for our hearts. God has blessed us with vegetables like collards greens, cabbage, garlic, onions, tomatoes, carrots, green peppers; and so much more that will cause the body and the heart to grow healthy and strong. Kudos to you Arianna! You are very knowledgeable about a lot of good and godly things.

When we eat good and wholesome lean meats, nuts, fruits, and vegetables, we still have to exercise for the heart. God didn't create His people to be lazy bodies. Allow me to share some wisdom that my dad once shared with me. He said that when he was my age, that they didn't sit around all day playing video games; they were more active. My dad said that they did things like play basketball or football; and he enjoyed playing those sports. Especially, basketball. Him and my uncle Steven were the best. He also said that little girls, like myself, would participate in games like pitty-pat and double-dutch or they would hula hoop; and the younger guys would go to the nearest grocery store and help the elderly folks with their grocery bags or offer to cut their grass free of charge. The little girls like myself would help their mothers or grandmothers around the house.

"They were always doing something active and fun." Things like going to amusement parks like Disney World, Six Flags, Wet willy's, Kings Dominion, or Bush Gardens help to keep our bodies moving and growing. Being young is a plus because our minds are fragile and like a sponge. Just as sure as a sponge absorbs liquids, our fragile minds will constantly absorb knowledge very quickly because we are still in our growing stages.

This sponge-like ability to pick up knowledge is also why we have to be extra careful about what we learn along the way. Whether it's from video games that are being played by kids our age and up, or some of the bad influences that we see on the internet, tv, or even the music that we listen to on the radio or iPhones. If it is bad for us, we must not pay any attention to it; because those negative messages will enter our minds. By entering our fragile minds, these messages just might corrupt our hearts.

One's thinking formulates one's behavior. Meaning, if you have bad and evil thoughts in mind, that is the way you will act. The bad and ungodly things that have entered one's mind cause the heart to harden. So, when the heart has become hard, it corrupts the love and care that goodness caused to once exist in one's heart. Suddenly a good heart become a bad heart, which we all know that a bad heart is detrimental to the MIND, BODY, and SOUL! Therefore, good and pleasurable thoughts will result in good and pleasurable actions. We should always keep our hearts pure by possessing Godly thoughts

By doing what our hearts and minds need, we will remain undiluted and keep the genuine purity that God gave to each and every human being from birth. That is why we have to continue to focus our attention inward toward the heart, the mind, and the soul. They all tie in as one. The heart was created to love God yourself, your parents, as well as all of God's creations. Your soul was created to spiritually whisper to God with your entire self; and your mind is to help you make Godly decisions in your actions. To worship God with our entire being is the duty of all human beings. God didn't create us for any other reason. However, by His will and His mercy for us, we are allowed to do other things. He allowed us to use our intelligence to continue to learn about Him and His creations. God's creations are beautiful, but most of the time we're too busy passing through life to stop for a moment and really observe and marvel over our surroundings. If we were to become aware of God's creations, then we would begin to acquire the necessary love in our hearts to appreciate life as a whole.

Did you all know that nature devotedly obeys God? The clouds, the sun, the moon, the stars, the rain; the entire planet earth all faithfully obeys God. He created it that way; and in addition, all human beings depend on nature. We depend on the clouds in the sky for rain. We rely on the sun for its heat and light. All glories in its privilege of service and obedience to God.

With all of nature obeying God, why shouldn't we? It is part of our original nature and we must respond to it as all beings do. If God's earth, sky, rain, sun, and moon can all devotedly obey God, then we as human with a heart should not only obey and love God's command and creations… we should also have love for his wonderful earth as well

The earth is one of God's one of the many fortunes God has blessed us with. We depend on it in so many ways. Even ways that we are probably not familiar with recognizing. A few chapters back, I said that my ancestors are from Africa; and were once kings and queens, as well as little princes and princesses. On my ancestors' continent, God's earth produces precious gems such as diamonds, and gold. Africa is not the only and with God's fortune. Earth also produces other minerals and natural elements such as lumber, copper, coal, rubber, rhodium, and oil. All of which are harvested or mined then refined and transformed into useful end products. Even though you might see poverty in Africa and other countries, there are still a riches a beautify on that continent and others.

You may be wondering, if our African brothers and sisters are living on wealthy land and surrounded by God's precious gems like diamonds and gold, then why are so many of God's people starving and living in broken down villages and forced to drink polluted water? You might even be wondering how could America be the richest country in the world when Africa has been blessed with a lot of God's precious gems and resources? This is because those that explored God's land for His resources don't distribute the wealth amongst the African people. Big million-dollar corporations that have a strong appetite for those resources excessively dig into God's earth for oil, gold and diamonds, and other raw materials. Then those raw materials are reproduced and replenished and traded or sold on the market for money or stocks. While that is happening, the African people are left to with little to nothing. So, now when you turn on your television or look on your computer or iPhone and so happen to see the ungodly sight of God's suffering people, you will have the knowledge of how it all happened and continues to take place.

The next question may be, why would someone do such ungodly things to God's earth, and why to God's people? Because their hearts are absent of God, love and care. Those are the ingredients for a heart of Gold!

Having a heart of gold means you possess a pure heart that includes all three ingredients that I have just mentioned above. We must never allow man to separate our heart from God by corrupting the it for selfish or material reasons amongst other things that are ungodly, like greed. So, we as the generation of change, must keep our pure and solid hearts and never let the evils of this world separate it, or corrupt it. We will keep our hearts, minds, bodies, and our souls pure, godly, and as one with God who created it. Now allow me to give my precious family some righteous solutions to keep it that way for now and forever, If God wills!!!!

My daddy taught me how to express good behavior, proper etiquette and graceful manners and to love all of God's creations. He is my role model; and I know that he is smiling down on me from heaven for continuing his legacy as I proceed on my mission. Because of this, I want to encourage others to possess similar characteristics. So, that their hearts and minds will remain pure in this world -which is full of temptation and corruption. Did you know that the root of all good… good behavior, good manners, etc. is the heart? It's true! So, if we carry ourselves with good and decent manners, we will display a reflection of God in the eyes of our peers. Because God loves those that are kind, polite, humble, and modest in their actions. Even when we are around others. Everywhere we go, we must behave Godly! When we are in school amongst our classmates and teachers. Or out and about having fun with our friends; or at home with our parents… we have to conduct ourselves with good manners and good behaviors.

You must strengthen the heart with these characteristics if you want to remain Godly. If you apply this whole heatedly in your everyday life, you will be secured with a heart purified from all bad manners or deceit, corruption, as well as evilness! When we let evil intrude upon our hearts and minds, it taints the purity of our efforts and ruins our love and sincerity. Remember, God only accepts actions that are intended purely for His pleasure. So, when you do a good deed, do it from the heart and solely for God's sake! If you do it for any other reasons, your deed goes unseen in the eyes of God.

I have just explained the characteristics of a hateful heart, now I will explain the characteristics of a sincere and love heart. A loving heart is truthful and sincere. It does not cheat or deceive others. It isn't envious. It keeps promises, it has a good attitude towards others, and it treats them well. It is compassionate and merciful. It is tolerant and forgiving. It is easy going with others. It is cheerful and countenance, it has a sense of humor, it avoids cursing and foul language. It does not interfere in that which doesn't concern them. It avoids giving false statements about others, it does not converse privately with another person present, it isn't arrogant or proud. A loving heat is humble and modest. It does not make fun of anyone. It respects elders, the weak, and the feeble mind people. It repays favors, and is grateful for them! A loving heart intends to make people happy. It guides others to perform righteous deeds. It is easy on people and not hard! It is fair in judgement of others; a loving heart doesn't oppress or mistreat others; it loves all god's creations. It does not rejoice in the misfortunes of others. It is generous, and it does not remind the donor of its charity! Love is each one of us teaching just one other person what love is.

Chapter 6

Each One Teach One

*If we all agreed that we are equal as people, then why can't
we see what is evil ? I can't breath you taking my life from
me, I can't breath would someone fight for me....*

- H . E . R .

I have learned how to love; I have learned how to share. If I
teach someone what I've learned, then I learned how to care!

It's more than just learning about the ABC's, 123's, or the birds
and the bees! It's about learning how to love and teaching other what
you have learned. Whether it's about God, His creations, or the laws
of the land that governs God's people which guarantee their rights as
human beings... The key to unification is passing on the knowledge
we gain.

In my each one each one chapter, we will not only learn about
the importance of those wonderful things, we will also learn how
to share them with the world!!! Before we start, I must ask are your
thinking caps still on? If so, then you should be ready to use those
brilliant minds in an intelligent and Godly way! Being that we are
the generation of change, we know that our goal is to bring true
and real change throughout the world where it is needed for every
race, creed, or color. We are also fully aware that love conquers all
hate -which means that hate doesn't exist in our world. We all have
hearts of gold, so we are one pure and solid family; and we will not

allow hateful hearts to separate us from God's mission! Furthermore, each and every one of us will teach those who are ready to be on the same Godly mission that we're on. We are the ones to make sure America lives up to its promise! In order to do that, we must inform the people of what America's promise consists of.

In my generation of change chapter, we have already discussed citizens and the rights that we as citizens are entitled to. Now, I will briefly talk about the constitution of the United States of America. This constitution is the structure that guarantees those rights we spoke of. Of course, African Americans are supposed to be part of those people that they speak of in the American constitution AND the Declaration of Independence, -which declares 'we hold these truths to be self-evident that all me n are created equal'. This means not only men, but women and children of all races that are endowed by their creator God -who has given us unalienable rights including but not limited to life, liberty, and pursuit of happiness! That life that they speak of is to live and breathe on God's earth amongst His other living and breathing creations. That word liberty is to be free on God's earth with the same rights and privileges of any other human; and that right to pursue happiness is the enjoyment of the fruit of our labors so long as it does no harm and brings glory to our Creator.

These words of life, liberty, and happiness hold a lot of rights in our everyday life in America! If we are deprived of just one of those powerful words, then we have been deprived of the very existence that God gave us. By knowing these rights, we will make sure that they are applied to us anywhere on God's green earth. Especially, right here in America! If we claim to be an agent of change for the suffering people but we are not informing and teaching them about their constitutional rights, then we are not fit to say that we are leaders of God's cause. In the profound words of Malcom X, "We have to come to realize that no people can achieve freedom as long as their leaders lack knowledge and understanding regarding how the economic and political systems of the world came into being, and how they function today."

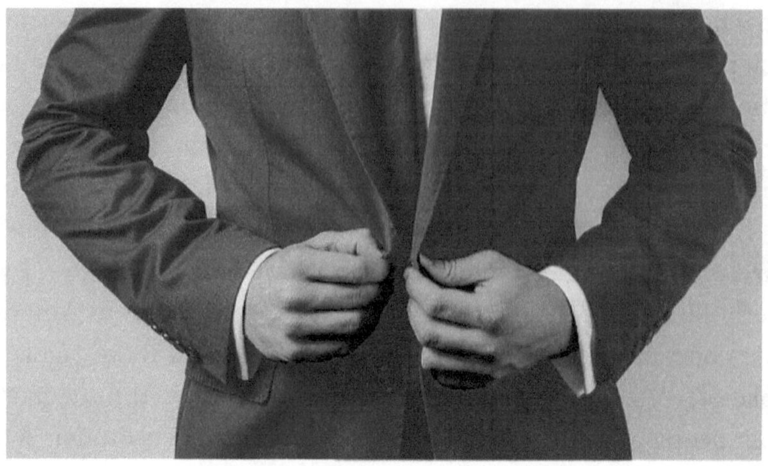

It's sad that we as kids have to witness a tragedy amongst loved ones or grow older and run blindly into racism or discrimination and all the inevitable evils that the average African American faces in this society every day. When I was out protesting with my friends and family, I saw parents with their kids my age or older experiencing the importance of protesting. Their parents were getting them prepared mentally, as well as physically for their future; because those parents wanted their kids to participate in something that their parents, and their parent's parents have been a part of for at least three generations. Advocating for change, trying to be that voice to be heard by the deaf ears and hardened hearts of those that are in authority who could make that righteous change for God's people.

Those parents were also preparing them mentally because that change obviously hasn't come yet. They were getting their kids mentally and physically ready for that horrible monster call racism! They were teaching their kids not to be scared or afraid in the least; and to deal with it in an intelligent and peaceful but stand-up way. This is a job as well as an obligation for our leaders of today. One who professes themselves a leader and fighter for change for his people must educate their followers about that same change they are actually fighting for. Real leaders go hand to hand with their followers; they lead by example. This doesn't mean shouting form a mountain top with no action behind all the noise. It means fighting in the valleys with those who suffer. As our brother, Dr. Martin Luther King Jr. also believed that a good leadership involves so much more than talking loud enough to attract the national attention. Real leaders are not self – appointed; but are chosen by the people. They are those who teach and are taught. They are best known by their solidarity, their willingness to serve and to suffer with the people; even to the point of their demise! Furthermore, Dr. King also believed that a true leader does not include their names during celebratory events in their honor. They are the people who aid the poor, empowering them to fight against the cruel conditions of poverty and police brutality. We must continue the legacy of those before us, for they are who sacrificed their very existence so that their children and grandchildren as well as future generations of African American children, could live free from getting cut down while playing on their neighborhood playground. All because the police might assume that a toy was an actual weapon!

Unfortunately, this is the very kind of police violence that happened to Tamia Rice -who was only 12 years old at the time. I'm only six; and I have lost my father all because of a fake 20-dollar-bill. Something that wasn't worth the paper it was printed on and that could have been received or spent without knowledge of its falsehood. Yet again, police violence has claimed another life for which God has blessed every child with; and that blessing is a father! You may say Arianna, I thought that this was supposed to be a kids' book? It is but this book isn't your average bedtime story. In this book, I have written the realities, as well as the lessons of life. I'm not sugar coating the truth by any means. I am only writing what God loves; which is the truth, and nothing but the truth!!! I advise that the truth should be told in every household. Especially, the truth about the realities of the criminal justice system in America!

We as kids will grow up walking God's earth with what we have been given and taught in our upbringings. Whatever teaching that we hold on to, will shape our thinking -whether that be positive or negative. We only react to what we have been taught. Therefore, the parent can give the reality to their children, and their children can give it to their children until justice and freedom finally ring true. Each parent must do their part in teaching a generation about systemic racism in this country that is built into the laws, the policies, the institutions, the inequities in housing, the health care, the education, the economy, and… yes, the criminal justice system. Honestly, I think this is where that ugly monster will stop right in his evil footsteps! I feel that with God's grace we are the generation to bring about that long overdue change that our enslaved ancestors and our beloved hero's and shero's fought and died for! Now, they will be very proud; because we have been carrying the torch of justice in a way that has never been done before. We are young, ambitious, fearless, and outspoken; and we refuse to give up on the fight for our respect as well as our equality in America! A country our forefathers shed blood, sweat, and tears for over four hundred years just to build. Discrimination, racism, and ongoing police brutality are the only thanks they get; but we are here to say with conviction, no more fluff and empty gestures will be accepted.

Instead of lip service from public show offs, this generation demands a real commitment to change. Policy makers still fail to implement true and just policies for God's people. They are still not acting as the constitution prescribes. So therefore, we have to create our own change. That change must consist of doing for ourselves and creating our own liberty, peace, and happiness on God's earth. As the great Coretta Scott King so beautifully stated, "Justice is never won, you earn it; and within every generation it goes away when a generation drops the ball. We can't drop the ball…"

The righteous and tender guidance of my wonderful mother, as well as the caring and helping spirit of my grandmothers and my father, along with the leadership mindset of my lovely aunt Bridgett, all add up to a potent combination. An instrumental force to spark a world-wide movement for justice. For that to become reality, we must bring forward proper solutions because the problem has already been diagnosed based on the unnecessary suffering and hardship, which are ongoing, and directly effects God's people! So, with God's help and our sincere plans to uplift ourselves as well as our communities nation-wide, we will indeed change the adversity into prosperity.

Here is a full sound proof solution from some of God's sincere servants who wish to bring change in various ways. These are the leaders who have vowed to be on the frontlines to help fight for justice, freedom, and equality for the ill-treated black and brown people in America; all while being that voice that echoes global change for every suffering human being on God's earth. One of those wonderful people that I passionately speak of are my Aunt Bridgett Floyd and she is my beloved father's sister. Out of her love for God and her struggling people, as well as to continue her brother's legacy, she founded the George Floyd Memorial Foundation to bridge the gap between the community and law enforcements. Her foundation isn't for talking sessions or false promises; it was created to bring forward powerful and meaningful police reform, engage nation-wide organized protests, implement voter's education, host community events, and educate the public on racial injustice. She intends to open centers that will be safe havens for young black men. My auntie also wants to start a second chance program that provides services for men and women released from prison -which I believe by the time this ink is dry and this book has been published, (by God's will) it will be up and running.

We are teaming up with other powerful movements, such as J.F.K.Q (Joining Forces with Kings and Queens) - a nonprofit foundation which was founded by Cedrick Lines. The foundation has several board members, all sincere and God-fearing men and women, who have dedicated their time and lives to ensure genuine prison reform for those who have been written off from society and labeled as failures. These fighters for justice among those incarcerated are Christopher and Sharlene Thompson (the founders of The Mile High Boyz Club), Topeka K. Same, Cedric Lines of Amongst Conquest/ My Brother's Keeper, Ferrone Claiborne and Terrence Richardson, the two faces of Not Guilty who were sentenced to life, and Kevin Williams -a board member of JFK. They are literally turning jail into Yale! JFKQ is turning prisons into colleges and universities. Their goal is to teach young men that they have the potential to be great! They are showing those young men and women how to turn their potentiality into an actuality by awakening the inner being to its true greatness! Thus, building the inner self through the mental process of mind cleansing and constructive engagement; transforming them from the so-called criminal mentality to an entrepreneur mindset. In meeting this goal, JFKQ will be equipping them with the requisite tools to be productive members of society and allow them to be released with the proper resources along with strategic planning for their futures, and a legit blueprint. These men and women will then be able to succeed in a free world, where presently the odds are stacked against them. They will become income earners, as well as productive mother and father figures and even role models in their respective communities.

I must say that this is very touching to me being that I can relate! My dear father was once an incarcerated black man who was blessed with a second chance to be a productive member to society. He made the best of the opportunity to start again and never returned up until God called him home.

So, I send my blessings to my auntie Bridgett, and the JFKQ foundation, for giving a helping hand to those who desire a second chance without being stereotyped. Afterall, they are kings and queens utilizing their efforts to aid and assist our brothers and sisters who are still incarcerated. Family! I would like for us to join forces as the princes and princesses with the known children of the parents who have been directly affected by mass incarceration inside and outside of prisons. Together, as a unified front, we can make a change. Our path to a brand-new reform starts in this very book. We demand police reform, we need police reform, God knows we do.

Hear me, this is much bigger than the police. Police brutality is as predictable as it is tragic. We will always have police brutality as long as we remain a nation who benefits from mass incarceration. "Systemic racism is the mass incarceration is the beast. And all beasts have to feed. The escalation of encounters between police citizens is the means through which the beast is fed." - Rev. Raphael G Warnock.

Until we break the monopoly the oppressor has on our minds, liberation is not only impossible, it is unthinkable, Therefore, we must strive on and utilize all resources at our disposal, until every suffering soul no longer cries out for justice, peace, and equality. There are 26 letters in the alphabet; if plan A or idea B doesn't work… then other solutions are available. So, we must try the whole alphabet A-Z, with ideas and plans to change the world. Also, for those who are dreaming about change and not putting action to dreams, you can apply the five W's. **W**hen **W**ishing **W**on't, **W**ork **W**ill. You can't think, wish, or hope for change; you have to work for it. It has to be accomplished one step at a time; while each one is teaching one until we are all on the same page with the word FREEDOM big enough for the world to see!!!

In chapter four, we talked about what love and hate are. We also talked in chapter four about how hate has caused racism; but I never told you about what racism means. Racism is a belief that one race is better than another. I know what you're thinking and I thought the same thing. If God made us all equal, then how is it that you are better than me or I am better than you? That can never be, because God made us all equal; and equal means that we are all the same.

Now that you know what racism is, wouldn't you all like to know where racism came from? Well, let's learn more about it. Racism has been around for years. In fact, racism was around long before you and I were born. Remember, racism is just a belief inherited from someone else that thinks that he or she is better than you or I because of the color their skin or for any other reason. Yeah, that's right, I did say because of the color of their skin! It doesn't matter if you are black, white, yellow, red, or brown; because we are all God's creation. God made us equal so we should never think that we are better than someone else. Racism is wrong!!! You should always love others, no matter what color they are. The same way that we can cure hate with love, we can cure racism with that same love.

For example, let's say that you are a little white boy or girl; and you see a girl or boy that isn't white. That boy or girl (that isn't white) tells you that they are hungry or thirsty, and you have plenty of water to drink and plenty of food to eat. Will you deny that girl or boy food or water because of the color of their skin? Of course not!!! Because giving that person food or water is an act of kindness.

Remember we said that love is to be kind and that love is giving? We can only begin to end racism by giving love! Imagine if you were that little girl or boy that was hungry or thirsty and you needed food or water. How would you feel if someone denied you food or water just because of the color of your skin! I know that you wouldn't like that. Neither would I! Things like this happen every day around the world. It's called racism; and you or someone you know could easily become a victim of racism. Be sure to talk to someone about it. Tell someone how that experience with racism made you feel. Never hide your feelings about it; and if someone you know was a victim, let that person know that everything will be ok. These experiences can be traumatizing. Give that person a hug, and let them know that you are there for them. Again, love is how we will cure racism.

Throughout the rest of this chapter is a few tests to see how much you have learned about love, hate, and racism. Answer the questions as best that you can. Whatever you don't understand, go back and read the chapters about that subject again. Or ask a loved one to help you understand the question.

Answer these five questions with the knowledge that you have learned from reading this book. Circle the correct answer.

What do racism mean?

    A. To be kind
    B. To love god's people
    C. A belief that one race is better than the others **What do Love mean?**

    A. To care for everyone
    B. To be kind to everyone
    C. Both to care and be kind to everyone **Who is God's creation?**

    A. Black and white people are God's creations
    B. Yellow and Brown people are God's creations
    C. We all are God's creations **Who is better than you?**

    A. A black and white person is better than me
    B. A yellow and brown person is better than me
    C. Nobody is better than me because God made us all equal

If I see someone that is hungry or thirsty, and that person isn't the same color as me what should I do?

    A. Deny that person food or water because of their skin color
    B. Give that person food and water and make sure they have enough C. Just give that person water

Below are 8 words that are mixed up. Unscramble the letters in order to spell out the worlds correctly. Write the correct word on each line that are numbered.

Evol inkd	1	2
Eacr odg	3	4
Oyj lquae	5	6
Aeht earc	7	8

Below are the words love and hate. Next to the word love, you have to write the 4 words that will describe what love is. Next to the word hate, you have to write the words that describe what hate is. Use the words below to fill in the blanks

rage, kind, joy, racism, destroy, peace, care, dislike

Love	Hate
1.	1.
2.	2.
3.	3.
4.	4.

To see how well you have understood what you have read, below are 7 sentences, and 7 words. Complete each sentence by filling in the blanks using the 7 words below the sentences. Ask someone questions if you don't understand how to complete this section.

1. If everyone in the world were to love _______________ wouldn't exist.
2. _______________ Created all things for a reason
3. Love is to be _______________ to everyone
4. We really need to start eating our _______________
5. Hate gives us a reason to _______________

6. Love is how we will _______________ hate.
7. The world needs us to be leaders; so that together we can begin to _________________ the world.

Kind, hate, love, vegetables, cure, change, God

If you were a victim of racism, write how it made you feel; and share what you wrote with someone you love. Write how you feel below. Remember, nobody has a right to judge you but God and he is forgiving. Be open to sharing your feelings with someone about how racism made you feel. You never know, you may be able to help each other see the promises of God.

____

____

____

____

____

____

____

____

____

____

____

____

____

____

____

Chapter 7

God's Promise

"I'm for truth, no matter who tells it. I'm for justice, no matter who it is for or against. I'm a human being first and foremost, and as such I'm a fore whoever and Whatever benefits humanity as a whole."

-Malcom X- Autobiography 1965

We are God's generation, on duty with Good. Accomplishing outstanding deeds, grateful, obedient, and divine; with a righteous mission from God. Please allow us to proceed because obviously we are running out of time!

The first and most important thing we must do is seek God's help in earnest prayer to keep us physically active. We must do this while spiritually and humbly trusting in Him to grant us the necessary means for the uplifting of the suffering people. We must ask to complete our mission without the interference of evil persons that wish to stop righteous progress for those who have witnessed countless tragedies and hardships around the world. For those who cry out for justice and peace but are constantly ignored or denied. We come to You, oh God, as helpers and obedient servants who are sincere and devoted to Your cause; which is a good, righteous, and just cause. We come to You because our elders are getting exhausted in strength; but have maintained their endurance to carry on. So, because our generation is young and we are the future, we must take hold of the torch of freedom until victory of change is won. It is our obligation and our duty, because we are God's generation, to make a difference.

I opened this chapter up asking God to guide us on the right path, and to keep us focused without deviating from our aim purpose. Because at times family, it may be those who possess evil minds and are heartless with bad intentions to deter us from the road to justice. There will be many factors and forces that will conspire to hinder or stop our movement. The greater the good one seeks to do, the greater the trials one must endure; and the worthier the goal of the good one seeks to do, the greater the efforts one must put forth to succeed in the doing of that good. I said that to say this… no matter what obstacles that are coming our way, we must jump over them like hurdles, with leaps and bounds. We are God's earthly Angels blessed with the power and determination; we have been given godly light that will not go dim. Since we have taken hold of the fight from our elders, there's no turning back because through my youthful eyes, God's people are still disenfranchised and victimized by poverty, structural racism, and environmental racism.

Did you know that there are millions of people of color on a daily basis that are being exposed to hazardous sanitation sites, such as toxic waste landfills that are in the heart of poor black low-income communities? We're not only in constant fear of police violence, being discriminated upon in banks or work places, under tremendous fear of remain unemployed. We also have to worry about the air we breathe all because we are located and housed in urban areas that have a high risk of pollution. We, as youth, have the right to live in safe and clean neighborhoods, as do our parents who have a God given right to live and work in environments with clean air and water. We, as youths, also deserve completely safe, hate, bias, and police brutality free places to live and learn; whether that be at home, on play grounds, or at school. It is so inhumane and ungodly to let a race of people face such harsh conditions while those in authority turn a blind eye to the very existence of the matters at hand. That is why our problem is no longer a "Black problem" or an "American Problem", it is a HUMAN problem!

The eyes of God are on America… Yet and still the nation capitol turns a deaf ear to the shameful injustices as if the Architects of the Republics who wrote the words of the constitution and the declaration of independence didn't write them for us Africans in America. We don't reap the same benefits that were written and signed on a promissory note; but it's obvious that the very same promissory note is just a promise! It doesn't amount to a hill of beans when it comes to black or brown people who are so-called citizens. Ask yourself… if the benefits of being a citizen don't apply to you, are you really a citizen? What nation or Tribe are you from? Everybody has a Nationality. Everyone that is, except for us as black people. We went from being called the "N-word" to being called "Negros"; from being called "Negros" to being called "Colored"; and from being called "Colored" to being called "African Americans". Even after the emancipation proclamation, we are still in captivity on so many levels. We are still in search for the light of hope for millions of black slaves in the ghettos of America. We are still shackled by the chains of racism in some way, shape, form, or fashion! What do the words emancipation and proclamation mean? Emancipation means to be free from the restraint, control, or power of another; to be free from bondage. Mentally, God said we are born free and with freewill; but in so many ways we had to be (and still need to be) set free. Proclamation is the action of proclaiming. Basically, we were supposed to proclaim freedom of the state as far as slavery in 1865. These words were individually (and together) meant to represent freedom and equality to every America regardless of color. Unfortunately, these promises fell short of their meaning and intended representation.

Because our society has become comfortable with ignoring every day protests, because the status quo has become accustomed to marches and rallies organized by established groups, I believe we have to approach these issues in a different way. They have never seen this form of unity around the nation, or even worldwide. This time, we aren't divided into small groups; people of all colors are protesting together for change. We are overrunning cities, stopping traffic and bring everyday life to a screeching halt!

I guess the Emancipation Proclamation are mere words; and June tenth is just a celebration. I say this because that very freedom that was proclaimed, paints a picture of an America that is failing to live up to its promise. We've all heard these words before, but I must reiterate. The America that we know of has not yet lived up to its promise as a new Jerusalem or as a home for all of God's creations. We are still on a lonely island of poverty and in the midst of a vast ocean of material prosperity in terms of the economic need of constitutional obligations toward its citizens; a battle against unjust laws and unjust enforcers. Martin Luther King Jr. spoke of it and I am speaking about it today. Nothing has changed. Still, no racial equality in your congress. Still, no racial equality in your courtrooms; nor in our schools or prestigious universities, Hollywood studios, or Wall Street businesses. Not to mention Silicone Valley. Racial equality doesn't exist in center banks, nor in your oil and diamond entities. It does not exist in your empires and television outlets, which are all built on racism and monopolized and utilized by the powers that be. When my people finally come together and realize this truth, every valley shall be exalted and the racism in crooked places will be made straight and equal. Then justice will rain upon the "have nots", because God said He would not help a person until they help themselves.

This struggle for Justice is beyond the police department. Dr. King had spoken that we need to begin asking questions about our society. We must help the dispirited beggars and that one day, we must come to see that a system which produces beggars needs reform. It means that questions must be raised. Who owns the oil? Who owns the iron ore? Why is it that people have to pay water bills in a world that is two thirds water? We have to start asking questions and demanding answers until we get results. We might be young; but we have the power of God to act wisely. God has given us one of the trumpets like when the walls of Jericho were overthrown; so that we may blow down these walls of hate. These walls that have been built to block love, peace, and justice for all.

With a strong change, we can set free those who caught years for liberty and equality. We have to be inquisitive about the realities of this country in which we live. I admit that it is a beautiful country; but we hope and pray that some of the people that are living in it become loving and just. I'm referring to the ones that have the desire to remain in authority with hatred and envy towards a suffering race that wishes to rise to the bare minimum level of equality. I am referring to those that sit in high places, I'm talking state and local government as well as congress and the Department of Justice who spoon feed us with mundane and temporary fixes and call it "progress". That's not progress by any means. Malcom said, "…if you have a knife that's been plunged into a man's back twelve inches and you take it out only six inches that's not progress. That is solving part of the problem; the damage still can cause penalization… even that man's demise."

Joe Biden doesn't believe in defunding police. Why; because he is pro police. He always has been. Him, and all the rest of the presidents that came before him; Obama, Trump, Bush, and Clinton. They all want America to be a police state. He called real reforms like adopting a national use of forces standard, requiring and enforcing body camera use and strict observation, and recruiting more diverse police officers. If the whole police department consisted of blacks in every department throughout the United States, this government would be quick to shine light on the issues existing within its structure. Like I said before, it is the heart and the mindset of that person the determines how they will perform in positions of authority. If they are not of good character, they will still oppress, apprehend, and even kill people for their own personal reasons; abusing that authority will come easily. Why; because they have already been systemically brainwashed by a system that teaches them that they are better than their so-called peers. A system that teaches them that these "peers" are nothing than hard nose criminals.

This is the average mentality of the black slave catcher/overseer. Cameras won't do anything but confirm what has already been taking place in America; and that is trigger-happy police officers murdering our black men; our black women; our black children and babies. Even after getting caught on camera for the world to see, the men and women are still getting vindicated in their kangaroo courts.

There are many solutions towards this issue. One of them is that we need to prevent 911 calls in scenarios where police should not be our first responders. That means serious investments in mental health services for people experiencing homelessness; that may also mean having social service providers respond to call with police officers. This solution works well in theory until we realize that there is another issue needing solutions first. Just think about that suggestion for a brief moment. Who do you think is going to be the first responders before the 911 or police are called? Nine times out of ten, it's the very same brainwashed individuals that are working for the exact same system that is designed to harm us by incarceration or death!

Remember that it's the heart and the mindset that defines a godly and righteous person. So, when sister Tasha or Uncle Bo is acting out due to a mental breakdown from some bad drug he or she took to try to escape the pain and poverty that surrounds them, and an onlooker feels that he or she is out of control and calls the cops or has driven up with one… that cop is justified for killing him because he is backed by a witness that is certified and trained to lie for their counterparts. The truth is, we have to recruit and train our own mental health workers; build our own mental health services, our own drug treatment and prevention programs. We must handpick our own social service providers because that is where we go wrong every time. We depend on their systemic brainwashed government and state workers and policies that aren't necessarily in our best interest. We make simple assumptions based on beliefs we have developed while dealing with the current system and the reality is that the system will always do what is best for the system.

A day after my uncle Pholonise laid his big brother to rest, he had a direct message for the lawmakers on Capitol Hill. He said, "Fix the criminal justice system!" It was a brief but clear and direct point made about the problem at hand. If we are to make any other lasting changes, we have to start there. His youngest niece would go further to say, "Fix the structuralized and widespread racism and bias behaviors in the justice system and as a whole. An unjust system that has been solely functioning for one race and one class of people will not bring about the outcome we need moving forward. This has been the country's customary and traditional way of doing things for centuries. Yes, we have modernized and many ways but the bottom line of inequality is the same. It still remains prejudicial within a structuralized broken system.

We have now elected (the 46th president) Mr. Joe R Biden Jr., who said that America "has a bias and a racist structural system that needs to be fixed in every department within its structure". He also promised that he will make sure that it's fixed on his watch "immediately" (once he takes office) Well, Mr. Joe… eventually, we will come to know if the words that you uttered from your mouth were indeed true and meant from your heart; or if they were mere empty promises in a typical speech of a Politian. We will also come to know whether or not you are connected with the heartless; or if you are with God's people who have hearts of gold. Only time will tell; but the time is right now! Freedom and equality need to happen now!

Justice needs to happen now! These promises have gone unfulfilled for long enough.

Forty-six presidents later, and nothing has changed. There are still broken promises coming from a broken system that only works one sided. The result is a country that is deeply divided amongst its people. A country that is one-sided with its laws; its education housing, and its economic system. This is a problem that obviously needs to be addressed. With that said, it doesn't take rocket science to know that when something needs be fixed, it needs someone that has the experience to repair that which is broken.

The American structuralized system is in desperate need of repair and reform. We as American people all function under (whether equally or unequally) the same system... despite the clearly different outcomes, measures and actions taken in the same scenarios with different races involved. As far as the average African American is concerned, it is an old broken-down racist system. What needs to be made clear and understood is that just like a body and how each organ works together to make a fully functioning healthy body, our society needs every part of it functioning properly to thrive. Every piece plays its own role in the success and growth of our country. If there is a malfunction, then before long there will be system failure.

The main organ in this case is the congress which is the master repairer, who have the remedy and the experience to fix which is broken. Of course, congress is backed by the president with his executive power. Then there are the American people, who are the blood of their system. They keep the main organ functioning; without the people, the very functions would cease to exist because we are the ones who vote for those cold-hearted senators on both sides of the aisle -who continue to ignore justice; but things have changed! Now, we are recognizing that we are the powers of the earth; we are the ones who God have entitled the right breathe, be free, and live happy! No laws can continue to get in the way of God's promise. The rights that God bestowed upon all of mankind.

In the United States of America, we have elected officers that have been sworn in and ordered to secure these rights. You see, governments are just instituted amongst men, deriving their just powers from the consent of the governed. Who are the governed with power to give consent? Mankind, which is God's people who have authority or the power. So, whenever any form of government becomes destructive of these ends, it is the right of the people to a alter or to abolish that structure and institute new government. With that being said, it is our duty to institute a new government, laying its foundations on such principles and organizing its powers in a form or fashion that shall seem most likely to affect our safety and happiness.

The facts have been submitted to a candid world. Undisputed facts that a history of repeated injuries, oppression, inherited racism, and prejudice have been unjustly inflicted upon the black and brown people of this country. It is obvious that our safety is compromised and our happiness has been turned into sadness, fear, and anger. It's clear that these are indeed genocidal actions that have occurred numerous times, and continue to occur throughout America. The sad part is, the government is failing in its obligation to prevent these harsh and barbaric acts from being carried out on a specific race of people. The government has failed to enact effective legislation, such as criminalizing and punishing acts of genocide/police brutality, amongst other mistreatment and crimes against humanity. We, the generation of change, are calling for accountability to prevent further atrocities against people of color. People who that have the same right to live and breathe in this country as any other race of people -without being deliberately targeted just because of the color of their skin. Justice is needed now; and that means justice for all. This is a matter concerning all humanity! God does not like that ugly monster called racism and we have to zoom in and focus on uniting to create a better world for future generations.

CHAPTER 8

Zoom In

Zoom has become one of the most popular video meeting services since the pandemic -which has forced people to work, learn, and socialize virtually- started. I want to take zoom on a whole different level, by using it as a tool to bring unity and love while having deep discussions about the facts of life. My Generation of Change methodology is to open a frank and constructive dialogue about racism. We are taking meaningful steps to stop the spread of hate by banding together with the goal of building awareness about the very hate that is tearing of apart. This, along with racism and the pain and suffering it causes, all while giving sound solutions on how to defeat these issues. Building a mass communication base amongst parents, children, teachers and friends, as well as other outside focuses that play an important role in ending the hatred that has separated the American people for centuries is our main goal. The time to stand in virtual solidarity with the generation of change family is now. The plan is to put into place a routing of sessional live streaming with the generation of change panelist, sharing stories and problem solving, in addition to exchanging ideas and discussing plans on the issues at hand. This is a means of channeling our youthful energy towards something positive and constructive, showing a symbol of peace and bravery. We can do it, family! With good intentions and solid gold hearts, we can truly change the world! God will put a shield of protection and love around us as we come together against those that undermined the untapped power of the youth.

We are today's voice. We are tomorrow's example. We are the generation or change that are reaching out the youth on social media, zoom, and other digital platforms giving us an opportunity to reach a broader and more diverse group of other young people. This will be a national and international discussion on racial equality, human rights, and justice, addressing the effects of systemic racism and discrimination against people of color. It will show other races -in particular, our European brothers and sisters, that we can come together with a just cause. It is a way for our generation to connect and share powerful and wonderful things with each other from grass roots to foreign shores. We will be able to accomplish all this while preparing everyone in attendance to be creative and resilient leaders.

How powerful it is to do things collectively? Zoom In is not only the opportunity to unite with people all over the world, but it is also a way to be the change. We are the building block. We will create change by having those sincere conversations with people that don't look like me but share the same ideology as I do and have similar love in their heart for all people. It is something that's much needed in the wake of all the police brutality, and white supremacy resulting is death and injury all over the world. We could converse about building a community of our own while learning and highlighting the things we need to know. We can end up changing it all by using video conferencing apps to being about peace, love, and unity and learning to live a knowledgeable and healthier life together. We will be committed to working in partnership to help our communities connect, act, and thrive towards bridging the gap from suburban to urban neighborhoods and connecting people that live in them.

The 2020 election has exposed the separation that our country is suffering. That is why we as kids have to be the examples and leaders toward unity. We have to be the ones to remove or fill the spots in the legislative positions to seat only those who hold up justice and equality for the people. We must remove or fill the spots of those that are in economic positions of power currently held by those who deprive people of color meaningful bank loans or high ranking executive corporate positions. We must remove or fill the spots of those that are in authority, or in the judicial system who are abusing their power with the miscarriage of justice towards a certain race of people. We as a country must strive to do better towards its citizens. Especially, its minority citizens! We can't simply neutralize them with police brutality, prosecution, or incarceration. We must pledge to lend our talents, our resources, and our power to continue to change the world, as my beloved father did. We must come together as a nation to make a firm stand against racism and hatred! This is our solemn obligation to God and His people. Brave and ambitious generation of today and tomorrow, we don't want to win… we want to make the change the world needs.

Chapter 9

Change Makers

In order for us to make change, we must put ourselves in a position to do so. There are so many people suffering because of the fact that some people that have the jobs to make a difference in this country don't utilize their occupations as they should. This could be because of hate, racism, political influence, or a lot of other reasons. This is why I have prepared a list with several occupations that me and my generation of change family could choose to become so that that the positions that we hold in the future could contribute to us making the change that is needed.

Among these crucial positions are the following occupations. Doctor, dentist, vet, scientist, firefighter, school teacher, basketball player, baseball player, football player, tennis player, acting, musicians, famer, journalist, governor, city council, mayor, congressman, supreme justice, lawyer, president. Engineer, coder.

Did you select the occupation that you desire? If you have, remember this… in order for you to get the job that you picked, you will have to stay in school so that you could get the education and the skills needed to acquire that job. We have a lot of work to do! Are you ready be a change maker? I know I sure am!

Every job that is listed above can have a Godly and positive effect on the lives of the people that are suffering around the world! In fact, if we were to obtain these jobs, we could cause a positive and life changing affect for all of Gods creations, as well as for the worlds itself. However, every person living can be a change maker. Remember, you are never too young, too old, or too anything else to make a difference! Being that we are God's helpers, we would have the opportunity and obligation to contribute to the wellbeing of others. We have the privilege to make the changes that we see as being necessary for this world. So, help a friend, help a stranger, try to understand a different culture. Every deed big and small counts! Go out there and make a difference, be the change in the making. Be thee change daddy's death ignited!

WE ARE NOT TRYING TO WIN WE'RE TRYING TO CHANGE THE WORLD.